T0088400

Jazz Songs of Innocence

Bob Chilcott

for SSA, piano, and optional bass and drum kit

Contents

1. Piping down the valleys wild 3
2. The Lamb 8
3. The Little Boy Lost/The Little Boy Found 12
4. The Echoing Green 24
5. The Divine Image 30

MUSIC DEPARTMENT

OXFORD
UNIVERSITY PRESS

Composer's note

Jazz Songs of Innocence is the second jazz-influenced work that I have written for the Crescent City Choral Festival in New Orleans, and I am grateful to Cheryl Dupont, the conductor of the New Orleans Children's Chorus, and all the choirs at the Festival in 2011 for bringing the piece to life.

In these settings the piano part can be played exactly as written, or, equally, the pianist can improvise freely around the given lines. I would encourage the addition of bass and drums, and indeed of any other instruments that would work within the stylistic parameters of the piece.

The poems used in this collection are taken from *Songs of Innocence* by William Blake, and date from around 1788–9. They reflect not only thoughts unaffected by the burden of worldliness, but also timeless themes of wisdom and humanity.

Duration: *c.*16 minutes

OXFORD
UNIVERSITY PRESS
Great Clarendon Street, Oxford OX2 6DP, England

Oxford is a registered trade mark of Oxford University Press in the UK and in certain other countries

© Oxford University Press 2012

Bob Chilcott has asserted his right under the Copyright, Designs and Patents Act, 1988, to be identified as the Composer of this Work

Database right Oxford University Press (maker)

First published 2012

All rights reserved. No part of this publication may be reproduced, stored in a retrieval system, or transmitted, in any form or by any means, without the prior permission in writing of Oxford University Press, or as expressly permitted by law. Permission to perform in public and/or to exploit a recording of this work should be sought from a local performing right or mechanical copyright licensing organization, as appropriate, or by contacting Oxford University Press. Enquiries concerning reproduction outside the scope of the above should be directed to the Music Rights Department, Oxford University Press, at music.permissions.uk@oup.com or at the address above

ISBN 978-0-19-338156-8

Music and text origination by Enigma Music Production Services, Amersham, Bucks
Printed in Great Britain on acid-free paper by Halstan & Co. Ltd, Amersham, Bucks

to Cheryl Dupont and the New Orleans Children's Chorus for the Crescent City Choral Festival, 2011, with thanks for ten years of joyful collaboration

Jazz Songs of Innocence

1. Piping down the valleys wild

William Blake (1757–1827)

BOB CHILCOTT

*The piano part can be played as written or used as a guide. Bass and drum kit can join *ad lib.*

© Oxford University Press 2012. Photocopying this copyright material is ILLEGAL.

Printed in Great Britain

9
cloud I saw a child, And he laugh - ing said to me: 'Pipe a
cloud I saw a child, And he laugh - ing said to me: 'Pipe a
13
unis.
song a - bout a lamb.' So I piped with mer - ry cheer, 'Pi - per,
song a - bout a lamb.' So I piped with mer - ry cheer, 'Pi - per,
17
S./A.
(unis.)
pipe that song a - gain.' So I piped; he wept to hear.

21
25
f bright
(unis.)
'Drop thy pipe, thy hap - py pipe; Sing thy songs of hap -
28
- py cheer.' So I sung the same a - gain, While he wept with joy to hear.

32
S. 1
S. 2
'Pi - per, sit thee down and write In a book that all may read—'
A.
'Pi - per, sit thee down and write In a book that all may read—'
36
unis.
So he van - ished from my sight. And I plucked a hol - low reed,
So he van - ished from my sight. And I plucked a hol - low reed,
40
ff
And I made a rur - al pen, And I stained the wa - ter clear,
ff
And I made a rur - al pen, And I stained the wa - ter clear,
ff

44
unis.
And I wrote my hap - py songs Ev - 'ry child may joy
And I wrote my hap - py songs Ev - 'ry child may joy
48
to hear, ev - 'ry child may joy
to hear, ev - 'ry child may joy
52
to hear, ev - 'ry child may joy to hear.
to hear, ev - 'ry child may joy to hear.

2. *The Lamb*

William Blake (1757–1827)

BOB CHILCOTT

© Oxford University Press 2012. Photocopying this copyright material is ILLEGAL.

8
Soft - est cloth - ing wool - ly bright;
Gave thee such a ten - der voice,
mp
mp
10
Mak-ing all the vales re - joice,
mak - ing all the vales re - joice:
13
Lit-tle Lamb, who made thee?
Dost thou know who made thee?
p
p

*To avoid dividing the alto section, the upper alto line may be sung by the second sopranos.

23
mf ma dolce
I a child and thou a lamb, We are called by his name, we are called by his name.
mp
child oo
mf ma dolce
we are called by his name,
mf ma dolce
26
f
mf
Lit-tle Lamb, God bless thee, Lit-tle Lamb, God bless thee.
unis.
f
mf
his name. Lit-tle Lamb, God bless thee, Lit-tle Lamb, God bless thee.
f
mf
29
p
rit.
oo God bless thee.
p
oo God bless thee.
rit.
p

3. *The Little Boy Lost/The Little Boy Found*

William Blake (1757–1827)

BOB CHILCOTT

© Oxford University Press 2012. Photocopying this copyright material is ILLEGAL.

13
mf
Speak, fa - ther, speak to your lit - tle boy, Or else I shall be
mf
19
mp
lost.'
mp
23
27
S. 1
S. 2
mp
'Fa - ther, fa - ther, where are you
A.
mp
'Fa - ther, fa - ther, where are you go - ing?

31
go - ing? Oh do not walk so fast.
Oh do not walk so fast.
35
mf
ah
Or else I shall be
mf
Speak, fa - ther, speak to your lit - tle boy, Or else I shall be
mf
41
mp
lost.'
oo
mp
lost.'
mp

45
mp
oo
The
mp
The
49
unis.
S.
mf
A.
night was dark, no fa - ther was there, The child was
mf
54
unis.
mp
wet with dew. The mire was deep, and the
mp
59
mf
S.
A.
unis.
child did weep, And a - way the va - pour flew.
mf

64
mp
'Fa - ther, fa - ther, where are you go - ing?
mp
69
Oh do not walk so fast.
mf
Speak, fa - ther,
mf
74
speak to your lit - tle boy, Or else I shall be
79
mp
lost.'
mp

83
87
unis. mp
1/2
Fa - ther, fa - ther,
A.
mp
Fa - ther, fa - ther,
91
Fa - ther, fa - ther,
Fa - ther, fa - ther,

95
unis. p dim.
Fa - ther, fa - ther.
p dim.
unis.
Fa - ther, fa - ther.
p dim.
pp
100
Expressive ♩ = c.56
A.
p sost.
104
ALTOS p dolce espress.
mp espress.
The lit-tle boy lost in the lone - ly fen, Led by the wand'r - ing light, Be-gan
108
p
to cry, but God ev - er nigh Ap-peared like his fa-ther in white.
mp espress.
p sost.

112
p dolce espress.
oo
A.
p dolce espress.
He kissed the child and by the hand
116
mp espress.
oo
ah
mp espress.
led,
And to his mo - ther brought,
Who in sor - row pale through the
mp espress.
120
poco rit.
p
oo
her lit - tle boy weep - ing
p
lone - ly dale
Her lit - tle boy weep - ing sought,
her lit - tle boy weep - ing
poco rit.
p

124
a tempo
sought.
pp
sought.
pp
a tempo
pp
129
Tempo I
S./A.
mp
133
unis. mp
'Fa - ther, fa - ther, where are you go - ing?
137
Oh do not walk so fast.

141
mf
Speak, fa - ther, speak to your lit - tle boy, Or else I shall be
mf
147
mp
lost.'
mp
151
155
S. 1
S. 2
mp
'Fa - ther, fa - ther, where are you
A.
mp
'Fa - ther, fa - ther, where are you go - ing?

159
go - ing? Oh do not walk so fast.
Oh do not walk so fast.
163
mf
ah
Or else I shall be
mf
Speak, fa - ther, speak to your lit - tle boy, Or else I shall be
mf
169
mp
lost.'
oo
mp
lost.'
mp

173
mp
oo
Fa - ther,
178
fa - ther,
Fa - ther, fa - ther,
mp
Fa - ther, fa - ther,
Fa - ther,
184
unis. p dim.
Fa - ther, fa - ther.
p dim.
fa - ther,
unis.
Fa - ther, fa - ther.
p dim.
pp
8vb

4. The Echoing Green

William Blake (1757–1827)

BOB CHILCOTT

© Oxford University Press 2012. Photocopying this copyright material is ILLEGAL.

13
S. 1
S. 2
sports shall be seen On the e - cho-ing green, While our sports shall be seen On the
youth time were seen On the e - cho-ing green, In our youth time were seen On the
A.
sports shall be seen On the e - cho-ing green, While our sports shall be seen On the
youth time were seen On the e - cho-ing green, In our youth time were seen On the
16
unis.
e - cho-ing green, While our sports shall be seen On the e - cho-ing green.
e - cho-ing green, In our youth time were seen On the e - cho-ing green.'
e - cho-ing green, While our sports shall be seen On the e - cho-ing green.
e - cho-ing green, In our youth time were seen On the e - cho-ing green.'
19
1.
f
2.Old
f
2.Old
1.

21b
2.
poco rit.
SOPRANOS & ALTOS unis. p
Slower and freer ♩ = c.96
S./A.
Till the lit - tle ones wea - ry No
mf dim.
p
24
more can be mer - ry; The sun does de - scend, And our sports have an end. Round the
27
laps of their mo - thers, Ma - ny sis - ters and bro - thers, Like birds in their nest, Are

30
S. 1
S. 2
A.
mp
rea - dy for rest; And sport no more seen On the dark - en - ing green, And
rea - dy for rest; And sport no more seen On the dark - en - ing green, And
33
unis.
sport no more seen On the dark - en - ing green, And sport no more seen
sport no more seen On the dark - en - ing green, And sport no more seen
36
poco rit.
Tempo I
f
On the dark - en - ing green. The sun does a - rise, And make
On the dark - en - ing green. The sun does a - rise, And make

39
hap - py the skies. The mer - ry bells ring To
hap - py the skies. The mer - ry bells ring To
41
unis.
wel - come the Spring. The sky - lark and thrush, The
wel - come the Spring. The sky - lark and thrush, The
43
birds of the bush, Sing loud - er a-round, To the bells' cheer - ful sound, While our
birds of the bush, Sing loud - er a-round, To the bells' cheer - ful sound, While our
gliss.

46
sports shall be seen On the e - cho-ing green, While our sports shall be seen On the
sports shall be seen On the e - cho-ing green, While our sports shall be seen On the
49
unis.
ff
e - cho-ing green, While our sports shall be seen On the e - cho-ing green,
ff
e - cho-ing green, While our sports shall be seen On the e - cho-ing green,
52
unis. fff con forza
On the e - cho-ing green.
fff con forza
On the e - cho-ing green.
ff
fff

5. The Divine Image

William Blake (1757–1827)

BOB CHILCOTT

© Oxford University Press 2012. Photocopying this copyright material is ILLEGAL.

13
mf
- tress, And to these vir - tues of de - light Re -
mf
- tress, And to these vir - tues of de - light Re -
mf
16
p dolce
poco rit.
unis.
- turn their thank - ful - ness, re - turn their thank - ful - ness, their thank - ful -
p dolce
- turn their thank - ful - ness, re - turn their thank - ful - ness, their thank - ful -
poco rit.
p dolce
19
a tempo
poco rit.
- ness.
- ness.
a tempo
poco rit.

23
a tempo
p
mp
For Mer-cy, Pi - ty, Peace and Love Is God our fa - ther
For Mer-cy, Pi - ty, Peace and Love Is God our fa - ther
a tempo
mp
26
mf
dear, And Mer - cy, Pi - ty, Peace and Love Is
dear, And Mer - cy, Pi - ty, Peace and Love Is
mf
29
p dolce
poco rit.
unis.
Man his child and care, is Man his child and care, Man his child and
Man his child and care, is Man his child and care, Man his child and
poco rit.
p dolce

32
a tempo
care.
care.
a tempo
3
mp
36
mf
For Mer - cy has a hu - man heart, Pi - ty a hu - man face, a
mf
For Mer - cy has a hu - man heart, Pi - ty a hu - man face, a
mf
39
hu - man face, And Love, the hu - man form di - vine, And Peace, the hu - man
hu - man face, And Love, the hu - man form di - vine, And Peace, the hu - man

42
dress, the hu - man dress. Then ev - 'ry man of
dress, the hu - man dress. Then ev - 'ry man of
f
f
f
45
ev - 'ry clime That prays in his dis - tress,
ev - 'ry clime That prays in his dis - tress,
48
Prays to the hu - man form di - vine: Love, Mer - cy, Pi - ty, Peace, Love,
mf dim.
unis.
Prays to the hu - man form di - vine: Love, Mer - cy, Pi - ty, Peace, Love,
mf dim.

51
poco rit.
a tempo
Mer - cy, Pi - ty, Peace.
Mer - cy, Pi - ty, Peace.
poco rit.
a tempo
mf dim.
p
54
poco rit.
a tempo
p dolcissimo
And all must love the
p dolcissimo
And all must love the
poco rit.
a tempo
mp
p dolcissimo
57
mp
hu - man form, In hea - then, Turk or Jew.
mp
hu - man form, In hea - then, Turk or Jew.
mp

Processed in England by Enigma Music Production Services, Amersham, Bucks.
Printed in England by Halstan & Co. Ltd, Amersham, Bucks.